Noah
and the Flood

by Barbara Brenner
Illustrated by Annie Mitra

A Byron Preiss Book

A BANTAM LITTLE ROOSTER BOOK

NEW YORK · TORONTO · LONDON · SYDNEY · AUCKLAND

About the Bank Street Ready-to-Read Series

Seventy years of educational research and innovative teaching have given the Bank Street College of Education the reputation as America's most trusted name in early childhood education.

Because no two children are exactly alike in their development, we have designed the *Bank Street Ready-to-Read* series in three levels to accommodate the individual stages of reading readiness of children ages four through eight.

- ○ *Level 1:* Getting Ready to Read—read-alouds for children who are taking their first steps toward reading.
- ● *Level 2:* Reading Together—for children who are just beginning to read by themselves but may need a little help.
- ○ *Level 3:* I Can Read It Myself—for children who can read independently.

Our three levels make it easy to select the books most appropriate for a child's development and enable him or her to grow with the series step by step. The *Bank Street Ready-to-Read* books also overlap and reinforce each other, further encouraging the reading process.

We feel that making reading fun and enjoyable is the single most important thing that you can do to help children become good readers. And we hope you'll be a part of Bank Street's long tradition of learning through sharing.

The Bank Street College of Education

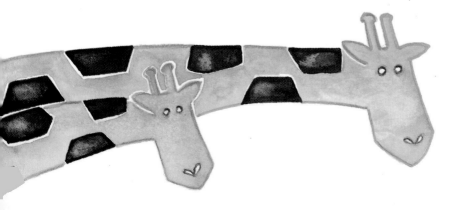

For Edith and Henry
—B.B.
To Lily and Noah
—A.M.

NOAH AND THE FLOOD

A Bantam Little Rooster Book / May 1992

Little Rooster is a trademark of Bantam Books,
a division of Bantam Doubleday Dell Publishing Group, Inc.

Series graphic design by Alex Jay / Studio J

Special thanks to James A. Levine and Betsy Gould.

Library of Congress Cataloging-in-Publication Data

Brenner, Barbara
Noah and the flood / Barbara Brenner;
illustrated by Annie Mitra.
p. cm. — (Bank Street Ready-to-Read)
"A Bantam little rooster book."
Summary: Describes how Noah built his ark and saved
specimens of all the animals from the great flood.
ISBN 0-553-08133-0. — ISBN 0-553-35146-X (pbk.)
1. Noah (Biblical figure)—Juvenile literature. 2. Deluge–
–Juvenile literature. 3. Bible stories, English—O.T. Genesis,
[1. Noah (Biblical figure) 2. Noah's ark. 3. Bible stories—O.T.]
I. Mitra, Annie, ill. II. Title. III. Series,
BS580.N6B74 1992
222.1109505—dc20
91-20457 CIP AC

Published simultaneously in the United States and Canada

Bantam Books are published by Bantam Books, a division of Bantam Doubleday
Dell Publishing Group, Inc. Its trademark, consisting of the words "Bantam
Books" and the portrayal of a rooster, is Registered in U.S. Patent and Trademark
Office and in other countries. Marca Registrada. Bantam Books, 666 Fifth Avenue,
New York, New York 10103.

PRINTED IN THE UNITED STATES OF AMERICA

0 9 8 7 6 5 4 3 2 1

Now there was a time
back in Bible days
when the whole world
had turned bad.
Folks were mean and evil.
They cheated and stole.
They broke every one of God's laws.

Every one, every one —
they broke God's laws,
every one.

God was getting mighty sick of folks
breaking His laws.

God said to Himself,
"People in this world
just can't behave.
I'm downright sorry
I ever made them."

God said,
"I'm going to make me a flood.
I'll wash away
all the evil folks.
Then I'll start over
one by one.

One by one, one by one –
I'll start all over
one by one."

But then God
remembered Noah.
Noah and his family
were good folks.
They didn't steal or cheat.
They kept God's laws.

God didn't want them
to be washed away in the flood.
So God called down to Noah.

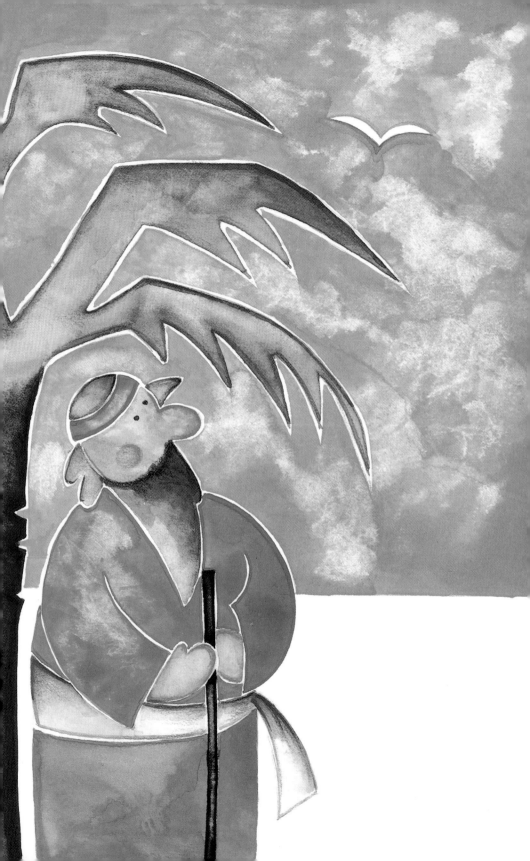

He said, "Noah?"
And Noah said,
"I hear you, Lord."
God said,
"Mind what I tell you, Noah.
There's a big flood coming.
Everything will be washed away."
"What about me, Lord?" Noah asked.
"What about my wife?
What about my boys?
What about their wives?"
The Lord said,
"Hold on, Noah.
Here's what I want you to do.
I have a job for you.
I want you to make an Ark."

"Get some wood planks.
Get a hammer and some nails.
Lay those wood planks
side by side, Noah.
Then hammer those nails in,
one by one.

14

One by one, one by one –
hammer those nails in
one by one."

So Noah went to work.
His boys Shem, Ham,
and Japheth
went to work, too.

They got some wood planks.
They laid them side by side.
And they hammered the nails in
one by one.
Noah and his boys
made an Ark.

Now that Ark was big.
That Ark was wide.
God looked down and said,
"Good job, Noah!"

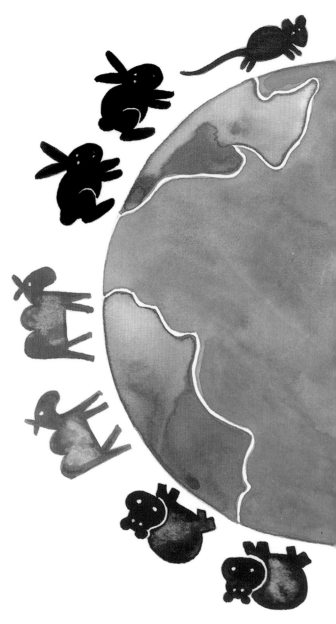

Then God said,
"Now, there's one more thing
you need to do.
Round up all my critters.
Bring them into the Ark
two by two.

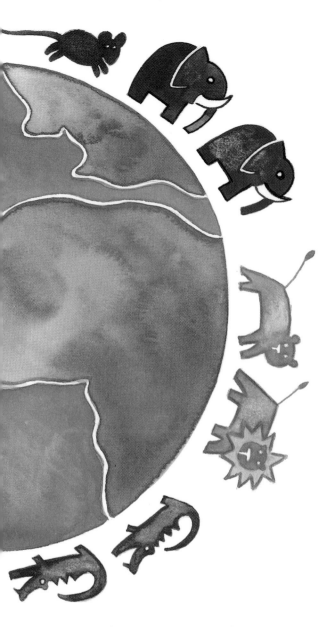

Two by two, two by two—
round up the critters
two by two."

So Noah rounded up the animals.
They came into Noah's Ark—
the big and the small ones,
the short and the tall ones,
the wild and the tame ones,
even some lame ones.

The crocodiles and the cats,
the zebras and the bats,
the hippos and the hares,
the monkeys and the bears,

the camels, lions,
and the gnus,

the tigers, snakes, and kangaroos—
they came into the Ark by twos.

Two by two, two by two—
the animals came
two by two.

When the animals were all
in the Ark, God said,
"Now, Noah. Here's one last job.
Put lots of food in that Ark.
You'll be feeding this crew
for a mighty long time."
So Noah brought baskets
and barrels
and jars of food
to the Ark.
He carried them in
one by one.

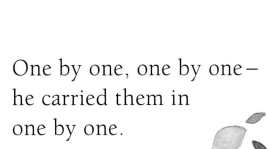

One by one, one by one –
he carried them in
one by one.

After all the food was in
and all the animals were in,
the people went in.
Noah and his wife —
and Ham and his wife —
and Shem and his wife —
and Japheth and his wife.
They went into the Ark, two by two.

Two by two, two by two —
they went into the Ark
two by two.

Noah said,
"I've done everything
the Lord told me to do."
And he closed up the Ark.
Right then it started to rain.
It rained for forty days
and forty nights.
Just as God had said,
every living thing
got washed away in the flood.

All that was left
of that wicked old world
were the critters and people
in Noah's Ark.
They sat there, two by two,
listening to the rain.

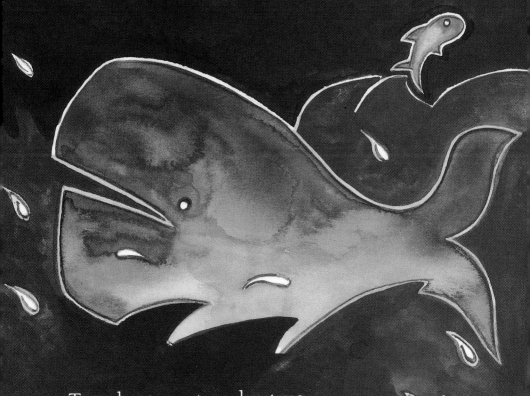

Two by two, two by two—
they sat there listening to the rain,
two by two.

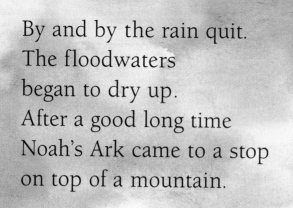

By and by the rain quit.
The floodwaters
began to dry up.
After a good long time
Noah's Ark came to a stop
on top of a mountain.

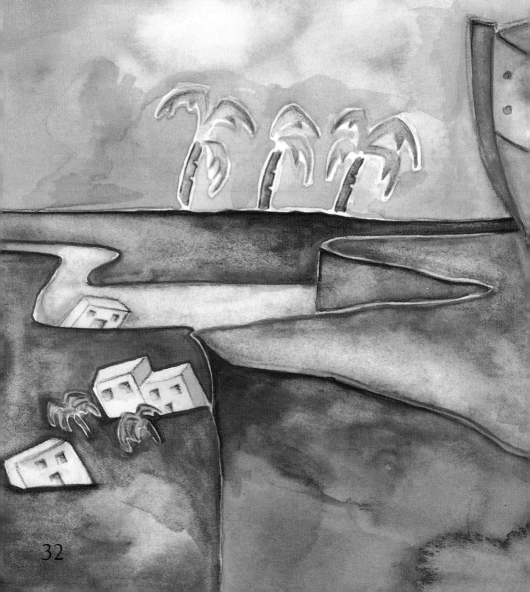

Old Noah opened
a window of the Ark.
He looked out.
"Looks like we're high and dry,"
he said.
"But is it dry down there?"
He sent a dove out
to scout around.
"Bring us a sign
that the flood is over,"
he said to her.
"Even if it's only one.

Only one, only one—
bring a sign, even if it's only one."

The dove took off.
The next day she was back
without a sign.
So Noah took her back
into the Ark.
After a week or so,
Noah sent the dove out again.

This time she came back
with a green olive branch
in her beak.
"Thank the Lord!" said Noah.
"That green is a sure sign
that the land is dry.
The flood is over!"

Noah opened up the door
of the Ark.
"Time to leave this tub,"
he said.
Noah and his wife—
his boys and their wives—
left the Ark, two by two.

Two by two, two by two—
they all left, two by two.

Then Noah opened the door wider.
The critters started coming —
the big and the small ones,
the short and the tall ones,
the wild and the tame ones,

even the lame ones,
the crocodiles, the cats,
the zebras and the bats,
the hippos and the hares,
the monkeys and the bears,

the camels, lions,
and the gnus,
the tigers, snakes, and kangaroos—
and all their babies!

Two by two, three by three,
four by four, five by five,
ten by ten, twenty by twenty—
the animals left the Ark.

Now God looked down
and saw all His critters
safe and sound.
He saw Noah and his family
safe and sound, too.

God said to Himself,
"I got me a new world coming!
And I promise, no more floods."
As a token of His promise,
God put a rainbow in the sky.

Now to this day
people say that every rainbow
in heaven's blue sky
is a sign from the Lord.

Every one, every rainbow —
every one is a sign
from the Lord.

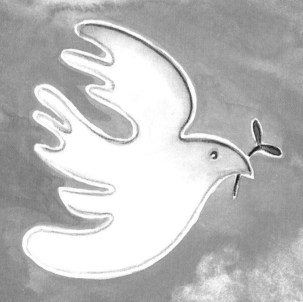

Barbara Brenner is the author of more than fifty books for children, including *Wagon Wheels*, an ALA Notable Book. She writes frequently on subjects related to parenting and is coauthor of *Choosing Books for Kids* and *Raising a Confident Child*. Ms. Brenner and her husband, illustrator Fred Brenner, have two sons. They live in Hawley, Pennsylvania.

Annie Mitra is the author and illustrator of *Penguin Moon* and *Tusk! Tusk!* Her magazine credits include *Seventeen, Essence, Good Housekeeping,* and many others. Ms. Mitra grew up in London, studied art in Paris, and currently lives in New York City.